Douglas Lochhead

TIGER IN THE SKULL

New and Selected Poems
1959-1985

Published by Fiddlehead Poetry Books & Goose Lane Editions Ltd.,
Fredericton, New Brunswick, Canada, 1986, with the assistance of the
New Brunswick Department of Historical and Cultural Resources, the
Canada Council and the University of New Brunswick.

Some of these poems have been previously published by McGraw-Hill
Ryerson Limited, Roger Ascham Press, The Aliquando Press, Oberon
Press, Anson-Cartwright Editions, *Canadian Forum, Dalhousie Review,
Descant, The Fiddlehead, Poetry Canada Review, Prism International,
Saturday Night,* and the Canadian Broadcasting Corporation.

Cover design by Julie Scriver

Canadian Cataloguing in Publication Data

Lochhead, Douglas, 1922-
   Tiger in the skull: new and selected poems 1959-1985

Poems.

I. Title.

PS8523.033T5 1986   C811'.54   C86-090128-9
PR9199.3.L63T5 1986

ISBN 0-86492-072-5 (cloth)

for Jean, Sara and Mary

Contents

The heart is fire

Now look the winter glide of doves
caught in a flurry of wing and white
downing the frosted fields of this December.

Like legions lost they carry the heart,
there it goes in claws of past and peril,
hot on the freezing breath of winter.

The heart burns in the talon cage
a fist of fire in the skin of cold
burning the night of this December.

Beyond the arctic limit lasts the heart,
now the claws and cage take flight
but the heart is fire, is fire, in this December.

Song

I grow as the wind grows
and cry with it;
flame as the wind flames
and burn with it.

I begin as the wind,
shaking before my time;
before anything resembling age
shakes my heart dry.

I rage as the rocks rage
and stay with it;
go as the wind goes
and die with it.

Pulse

The sea is at once
beginning and end,
the pulse around
and within.

In the wave
the pulse lives;
in the gull's wing,
in starfish
surviving the roll
and back of boulders
tossed and surf-blown
in the eye-blinking
Atlantic wind.

Pulse within pulse,
in the shell's rewording
of the sea's bounce;
here is the world's song,
the anthem in the bone
carried for listening
and hoping to the ear.

What stirs a bird

The narrow birth of sky
    through the half-closed window;
blue begun, beyond, who knows?
Under the stilting trees the earth
    begins to rumble in the roots,
to rumble with Spring inside it,
    and what stirs a bird
staggers a sailor long away, pinches a parson
    to look a little inward.

So the yellow on the eaves to glisten
    demands the sun.
It is partly a question of colour, the eye's message
    through the bone;
and what prompts departure in man and bird
    is all around,
it is all around.

Sunday rain at Ingonish

This Sunday morning we awoke to rain;
rain blowing in over Ingonish Island,
with wind knocking at the screen door
of the room waiting to be warmed
by hard wood fire. Immediate
the waves intersect as they roll in
at the Point. Behind whiteness of lips
a deep undersea green reveals itself,
a surprise in the rain-grey of such
a day. The green untells the depths
the waves toil from, the coils of energy,
of power, waiting power of hands held
supported by such muscles and spirit.
The deep green thresholds of the heart,
the poet restless, seething behind shades,
the owl in the thousand-fold leaves,
the unleashing of power and wisdom
in the wave, wing, and opening petal,
such is the world, the world.

In the lost forest

In the lost forest
the green trees
ape my silent dreams
like torn gods
from some strange history.
Their mute songs,
hollow in the wind,
are like the moanings of children
in a bombed city.

All this sound and silence
whirls suddenly
in the unreason of dreams
when the sun and wind
toss the lights and leaves about,
filling the eye
like the most fantastic
girandole.

They tell me these are dreams
and that the eye sees unreason
filling the white pages—
But in the moonlight
these dreams are my days,
streets are deserts,
and I ride a white horse
in a lost forest.

In memory of James Eagleson, R.C.A.F.

i.

In what glorious air
an acrobat he grew,
sailing circus boy
in his net of air,
confident,
setting the Mitchell always down
and running out for one
last bow. Roar
of engine and love a limit
he knew, he knew so much
the crew, no trapeze
was that high, they could not
swing laughing and tense
Berlin, Hamburg, Bremen,
a tangled run to Ruhr
and back to pile out like apes
swinging from harness into
the happy jungle of their own.
Face in a NAAFI mug
and letters from home.

ii.

Trip of hammer and hell
black eruption of sky
and shell in September sun
and a rattling chance to go in
low and come out
like swimmers.

In the eyes quickly closed,
in the captured light, there came
sudden heat of red and white
filling the cabins of their skulls
with its close warmth
dull and dry.

The left motor hit square.
And in that minute
of war and witness
they were headed down.

Recruit

You will sign here.

You will understand
    that this is the army,
    that there is an enemy somewhere
    and that social disease
    is where you find it.
You will about turn
    counting three, placing
    the left foot slightly at an angle.
You will salute all college boys
    and sons of merchants
    raising the right arm . . .

You will breathe slowly twice
    kissing the stock with right cheek
    before squeezing trigger.
You will remember the Bren weighs
    twenty-six and one half pounds.
    To change the barrel simply . . .

You will see that darkness is not always
    for love, but patrols,
    planned nightmares, where arms are words
    and the enemy a past-master.

You will write "X" in squares
    meaning for mothers, your heart
    is pure, and the socks fit well,
    and please send more cigarettes.

You will recognize the mortar's womp
    without holler, never digging
    your glory hole below trees
    whose branches catch strange birds
    in their hair.

You will listen to all men
    wearing ribbons.
You will listen to those
    who have seen the glory.

You will pray when no one is looking.

You will curl in fear, in the womb
    of your pounding blood,
    in your private bed of whittled thorns.

Nova Scotia fishermen

I feel
Dark occupancy of tar and net-lashings
Of fishermen whose barrels lie
Sandfilled and dry,
By whose doors black madonnas
Sift the eye-filled sea, stand by the slip
Where Ella II, Ruth III and ten others
Scape the surging swell of green
Of the great Atlantic still.

Men whose red-torn faces reveal
Breast intimacies of dawn and sudden
Spilling from the reeling room
To balance cabers in the sun
When pipes are blown in thin strainings
Of Scottish succession and Irish shock.

From leaning houses, men, whose sides
Diesel-driven in the sea lend four voices
In guttural protest of gulls
And wet falling from the storm.

I feel
Wild crying from their drunken nights
Dull oblivion in Sunday suits
Along the blue-road of white rocks,
Along their eastern sea.

Phoenix

Look beyond wind, beyond the tireless air
into red and reeling the sounding sun, there,
in the nightless spinning round, there lava-bound
the breath and bark of heaven flame and burn.

In the heat beyond heat, flame hotter and wilder
than flame, spread wings of a million summers,
torrid in time, day on day burning and falling,
there in the terrible close burns the final fire.

Look into the terrific centre, into the breaking wound,
pain burns beyond pain, beyond anything resembling hate,
there in the great white purity of ash, the image grins
and grows in the fanning flaming wings and head.

Day in summer

On the island the lovers lie
almost lost in the feathery mists
of the heat straining
from the tortured womb
of an August sun.

My boat lies off-shore
drifting with the river,
only its red floor-boards
between my tanned feet
and the deep blue grave
of the river.

The lovers lie as close as that,
on their little island of sand.
Between embrace they toss pebbles up
and wait for the splash
and the turning out of the ripples.

Deep in our days of heat
we sup up all the love
in the world. In my boat
there are garlands of blue-flags
wet and moist
for all lovers.

In the elms

In the elms
of my silent father's garden
the families of blackbirds
perch and hang,
caught on the branches
like lumps of coal.

Their starling chatter
in these sunless days
turns down the avenues,
those looking-back ways,
and splits the flakes of silence
like chips
from the most delicate of dreams.

This is the diamond time,
the cold recollection time,
and their chattering
is an intrusion
like death.

I place my life

I place my life
upon this rock,
against this sea
to breathe, to love
this fog-spilt air.

Deep in the rock
beats the salt heart;
under granite
the grey mother
prays in her folds;
her ancient arms
under the rock
in the castle
grey and pounding.

Against this sea
the land follows
a task of time,
the beach is white,
the threshold waits,
and the castle
turns to air.

I place my life
upon this rock,
my hands hark
to mew and cry
of sea-birds' lives
at the going down
of the rock.

Blackbird

Out of a quick dead sun
a blackbird fly,
sit out a feather-while
on a cherry treetop,
then down down
he drop
to river bank,
where he nose around
like old man on Sunday
outside a big hotel.

Drill Sergeant-Major

You are a khaki-strutting Ahab
anchored to the strict minute
of your barrack square
and your marking-time
is the heart beat of the sun.

How methodically,
and with what persistent tapping
you must have come out of the egg!

Little man me

Little day little dollar
little man me
home for five o'clock hello
to sit in far corners
fashioning a dream
a bit of daring fancy
over supper over wife
who is my love
and will be
until the dying day
when the ancient fathers
with some sad sorrow
will lower crying hands
in pity and rejection
little man little grave
little dust me.

Winter landscape — Halifax

A bright hard day over harbour where sea
in chips of white and blue speaks and toys, while
flurries of gulls spinning in wide deploys swoon
in sleigh-rides giddy and cold off government wharf.

At Devil's the sea spanks a winter's drum,
a hollow ballad and boom for sailors' throats
courting their winter mermaids battened down
somewhere off Scatari and heading home.

Now in December the wind leans rude and hard,
snow heaps and hides in the cormorant rocks,
and at the Citadel commissionaires
clap hands, stamp feet, turn backs against the cold.

Poems in a train — Newfoundland

i.   Having begun this journey
        on this train, from this place,
there is no return
        but the going forward:
the necessary details of seat,
        rest room, baggage, the infernal
borrowed camera hung against the heart,
        occupy the present and the eye's
warped future. Waiting to begin.
        Out of a window the platform
gives way to harbour inlet
        and a gang of boats
huddled out of the wind.

ii.   Everywhere this land
              suggests beginnings:
      the rude rock still dripping,
           the virgin air
      gulping with the first arctic touch,
           the animal forms
      gripping the pool edges
           where shimmering life
      gleams silver giving lip to lip,
           sex to sex,
      and the thunder of innocence
           rejoicing.

iii.   From the windows
          it is all around us.
       The great waiting presences
          of these surprising mountains,
       near and remote,
          assure our tomorrows.
       The wilful tricks of feeling,
          of light on their shaggy sides,
       of looks from outside piercing
          our own terrible eyes,
       all dissolve, all unravel,
          simply as clouds do,
       while these great round peaks
          stay, stay!

iv.   Almost a joke
             this jolting train,
    its name "The Bullet".
             Its bumping presence
    in the sky of my brain
             and in the sea behind
    is the elusive ring of you
             into which I plunge
    all fire, all closed eye,
             the rod renewing
    and the fire regaining.
             It is enough
    as the shifting land
             of this place envelops
    and flashes by at the window.
             How its oppositeness
    claims me. All.
    The dragging, banging presence
             of the wheels
    inevitable with the rails
             leading on,
    as we remember our quiet
             in that first,
    within each other—
             the all-compassing nest—
    like birds we flew to it
             while the witness stars
    threw down dimensions,
             measurements of love,
    we had not known.

v.   From this stop we run out
over the living lake toward the wide valley
and the living hard-top hills
as our feet scarcely touch
the silver thighs, the liquid cheeks
of the water. The sudden soaring
of an osprey flapping high and madly
stops the eye as we run
and what happens in the heart
unties the foot and we are loose
in this land. The sun shapes the shadows,
the details of the homecoming shore.

vi.   Newfoundland is made up
                    of children
        and stones,
                    and during the interval,
        children.
        Like starlings
                    they perch on fences,
        window sills, tail boards,
                    and agile as elves
        they greet the train's entry
                    into their inland day
        with curiosity
                    and so what!
        and as the occasion
                    for hanging and madly
        swinging from the eaves.

Monday

It was a start,
someone let in the wind,
rain and stars,
clouds to rage,
rocks to spring
from oceans;
we watched this great force
knowing nothing
feeling the spell
creating the word,
the word living
and we were
its breath.

The force found us
in maidenhood,
a discovery,
we knew no secret,
wind held no despair
no tears, no ecstasy
only its own
pure urging.

The genesis:
the lid of eye
in time to watch
a bud, remember,
believing in no future
unfolded its bloom
a beginning colour
in your hand
a rose for you
from this rock,
a beginning.

March landscape

Newcomers, restless,
March crows
fighting a wind
over strong woods;
the fields between
are rigid in white
with grilled furrows
and this day
breaks
from hill to hill
with weather.

Black and white
the woodcut land
suffers this wind
as it rides
the ruffled birds
over the maples
and long blown fields.

One last sight,
almost too distant for me
to hear its banging;
it is a windmill
turning itself
inside out
its wheel spinning,
each vane
a tin finger of sail
against the sky,
metal moon,
as the wind
plays and pumps it,
almost a pin wheel
gone wild here,
over an empty
farm.

At the Fair Grounds

At the Fair Grounds
at Indian Head, Saskatchewan:
now in progress
until June 16th,
there are
"refreshing, Biblical, realities;"
an old fashioned
tent revival,
a special kind of oxygen,
"meetings with a Heavenly Touch,
tent comfortably heated".
Yes, at Indian Head,
the planting done,
the spring wind still on the prairie,
Billy Evangelist,
Esther Accordion, Special music and singing,
Norman Songleader,
will be there to help you
heat the tent with propane
and a heavenly touch.

The announcements shout from grey poles
where the roads intersect,
and the prairie pattern,
the wheat green and six inches,
takes new sounds nightly
at 7:30, Sundays 2:30-7:45,
and while hawks hover,
and mice undo the new wheat
with their track world,
the tent fills with friends
who have come! to see! to hear!
Billy Evangelist,
Esther Accordion,
Norman Songleader
at the Fair Grounds,
Indian Head.

Poet talking

I want first to hear
something the sea says,
something the wind knocks;
touch, smell something
the moment has;
has for sage and suitor,
sailor, scholar, saint;
and when all is there
then I will take it
tell it again my way,
loud enough
to crack mountains,
live it softly
for children.

Tonight we are exhausted

Tonight we are exhausted:
the movers have gone,
the furniture looks shabby,
not worth the six hundred and eighty-five
dollars, transportation and storage.
My wife is asleep,
the children lie open-mouthed
in their beds,
and I retire to the July night
to sit on the back steps
with a beer, to listen for the waves,
for the surf-roll and the feel
on the cheek of the thin-spun rain.
Overhead are the same stars,
but this is not Halifax,
this is Millwood Road,
I say it out loud, Toronto.

And the way we die

And the way we die:
>you hear about it, read somewhere . . .
>I remember when my grandad died,
>they had an old Nash for a hearse
>and we walked behind it
>grey and important and learning
>to be sad. And that was death,
>with the image of waxen face
>and flowers and women in a scented
>room. They lost their thoughts
>in food the neighbours brought
>and throughout I never saw my Grandmother,
>but I heard her weep. And this was
>a way to death.

Across the park my children race the clouds

Across the park my children race the clouds,
overtake and wrestle them to ground
like steers, or they seize them
with skilled hands of fishermen
tucking a finger behind gills,
or stride proudly shaping them to size
and rowdy toss them like pillows
at me, at each other, and rather
than admire and note, they cavort,
little Rimbauds, crazy with doing.

Two secretaries

Two secretaries
in bathing suits
lie down to sun
on stretched out towels.

They see everything
about them; like owls
their heads never seem to move,
they control the scene.

Their special qualities
are appreciated, I move
no official vote of thanks,
but they are appreciated.

Like two flaming flowers
they grow stems and petals
rising suddenly away
still untouchable.

The child cries in the night

The child cries in the night,
it is with fever.
I look into my wife's eyes
and ask her, "How do we assume
this pain, this fever?"

My daughter's cheek

My daughter's cheek
lies against mine
and what it says
is full of hope
and the world grows white
with her touch.

A gull hung up on the wind

A gull hung up on the wind
        over Davisville,
sheering in from the Lake
        looking for spring stirrings
of worms and garbage;
        an eye looking down,
while I from the sea bottom
        reach through the cold green
to tie him with words;
        but with one phrase of wing
he circles and glides away and wide
        bound for Mount Pleasant Cemetery
where the May grass is long
        and private
        for his searching.

The soft doves appear

The soft doves appear,
     disappear,
     from the garden;
     through silken thresholds
     they glide, easy in air
     they slide down days,
     down times of coo
     and love and petals,
     and the grey and blue
     and pink shiver
     of their here and there
     is softer than dream,
     more mysterious, yet
     they are again here,
     in this very garden, look!

In the evenings

In the evenings
at the picnic tables
the new Canadians sit
studying their grammars,
the way into the new world,
some spelling out the words,
reciting phrases: "This is
the harbour. Please carry
your suitcase". Yes, this is
their harbour, and probably
they will go home for a glass
of wine from Palermo, after an evening
of new dry words, thinking
of old harbours.

Homage to William Carlos Williams

Old man Williams
        went to town
riding on a poem.
        Old Man Williams
is not really, and he has so many
        poems, all with saddles,
all going to town.
        He has started more races,
not only for poets,
        starting-gate to the blue
of his real tellings,
        his all over blue sky world
enfolds me and I dance and tell
        run humble and wild, a full-back
in a flush of flowers,
        startled by a rose, a rose.

Migraine

These waking days the raging tiger
    rips his claws along my brain,
    yet in his way
    he is bleating lamb, he is child,
    but this disease, this crouching danger
    in the bush is sharp, alive,
    is pain.

    Remembering, those who for me
    truly, truly are great is a help:
    (Hearne the onward explorer
    of the barren grounds)

    out there Hearne would lie awake,
    all above was night and sky,
    wet through in the blankets,
    tobacco and water for three days,
    only then did he consider
    the unsleeping stomach,
    the tiger in the skull,
    reciting Young's *Night Thoughts.*

October Diary 25/10

The track of it
I feel
a cold needle
from the summer past,
a thrush note,
    that is it,
    one silver line
    from a hidden vireo
    in
    summer woods.
There are ways
to say what
    I mean,
    cold,
    out —
    out of
    what is to come
    day to day
    nail to nail
    in the crate
    of the year.
And it will be cold,
    a splendid fury
    in a coil of wind
    and we reassure
    by arriving first.
    Beating what gun
    from
    what imaginary
    start-line?
One by one, word by word,
the tracks I saw
    last March
    in prowling search
    around
        the edge
    of Whitby Marsh,
    marauder,

the animals do without
the helping priest
we need,
no, the tracks
several days old, some
where the snow lay,
some in the fine chocolate
of mud flats,
definite,
the mission recorded now
and,
I will go at it
searching my ground,
living it down
to earth
as tracks
are marks
in the snow.
Another where am I?
what am I?
beginning,
all wondering
always
to begin —
and he did stop
in his tracks
and he did ask
in a dark room
after a girl. Maybe.
God, machine, animal?
What went wrong in the
pickle factory
when they put my lid on?
Here is my mask,
not knowing the answer
but having to plead
with the sea-wind
with the absence
of place,

                    and,
            and the presence
            of this kind
            of whirling platform
            anchored
            and swinging
            as we are,
            now,
            in a balloon
            of love
            (here it comes)
Love it will be
            and always.

October Diary 26/10

To be like (pause)
    the simile and metaphor
    yes,
    the only hard way
    to follow
    the unsame days
    the ascent
    from the mud
    into question
    one big one,
          should stop
          this machine,
      what? the face said,
      and it went
      that way.
Nobody on the farms,
    held together
    by faith
    and a helluva lot
    of booze,
    ever said to me
either around Atwood, Ont
or Scotch Settlement, N.B.
not Uncle Amos coming in
    market day
    with a rig full
    of eggs, big
    Scots ape of a man,
    all parlour and whiskers,
    once the week
    and he put in eighty
          years
    and I felt for his
          grave
    through the tall weeds,
          burdocks,
    a regular Graham
          Sutherland
    landscape, hard blue

over the field of
                spikes
and the fingers
picking the lichen away,
tracking the letters
chiselled on the
toppled stone
AMOS
in a lost settlement
Scotch Settlement,
N.B.
So it is. I was
the only one in the
                world
to remember him in a certain doorway
at a certain time,
                in a grandmother's kitchen
                and a bag (basket?)
                of eggs he had brought
                        from the market,
                        and he loomed out of my life
                        until I found the broken
                                stone.
Today, I began in a fret of stomach
                and the eyes full of fire
                but the old man and woman
                I met at 9:30 sharp
                were not liking their age,
                I doubt if they ever had:
                Doug. Angina. Do you know what
                                that is?
                Never grow old. Had they
                        been young?
                I was forty years with the Bell.
                And hated every minute of it.
                I hated to get up in the morning.
                Why did the poor bugger
                        stay that long?

And he is convinced he has
          more shadow
than the rest of us.
          So, it went easier
and I came to real death
          where they were cutting
          two hundred years
          of elm down
          ridden with the local
                    cancer
of Dutch Elm disease.
The old man, the amateur
          bookbinder
and the elm, and myself,
all wanting to be praised.
This is the animal
          in us?

a place near calling water

a place near calling water

I

a place near calling water
a place with hawthorn
a place with dried grass
a place with beaten ruts
a place with burdocks
a place with goldfinches
a place with jack-rabbit
a place with ice
a place where clouds begun
      hinge on a morning
      on a pin-map moment
      on a hint of dog
      on a walking stranger
a place of field
a field aloud

in that all things do continue

II

in that all things do continue
ALL THINGS THINGS THINGS ALL THINGS
GO ON TO CONTINUE THIS DAY THIS DAY

give my knees to brambles and to stones
FOR ALL THINGS THINGS THINGS ALL
THIS DAY THIS DAY AND ALL DAYS

give my hands a burdock flower
FOR ALL THINGS THINGS ALL ROLLING
IN WINDS AND WORDS ALL THINGS

go down sweet sweet rolling prayer
GIVE FOR ALL THINGS THINGS ALL
THINGS GIVING THINGS ROLLING THINGS

all this day of field and stones
ROLLING THINGS THINGS ALL THINGS
CONTINUE THIS DAY THIS DAY

again give help lend voice for
ALL THINGS THINGS THINGS ALL ROLLING
THIS DAY THIS DAY THIS DAY

a grin box days gone cold cloud down

X

a grin box day gone cold cloud down
PAST FINDING OUT THE GREATER MYSTERY
GREET GREET THE DAY LIFE GLORY

a suffering hand undoes a frown
THERE IS A SOUL A GRACE A GREATNESS
GREET GREET THE DAY LIFE GLORY

my kite wears now a wild Christ's face
THE UNWELCOME WIND SPELLS PAST O PAST
GREET GREET THE DAY'S GONE STORY

almost not quite the kite whips harder
ALMOST LOST THE SOUL AND PULLING CHRIST
GREET GREET THE NEW LIFE GLORY

He sings alone

in the ordered alignment
of branches,
the elm at edge
where the field falls down
to straight lake,
the red-shouldered hawk sits
and seizes without flight
the air
the solid place
of earth and weed
and head turning
in — feather — shoulders feather
makes his own song
a rattle of fear
in mole and mouse,
and in fear to be broken
where they listen
in pulsing blood and bone
to the song
he seems to sing alone.

Evening grosbeaks

What in their flock history
made them draw bright tags and ribbons
across our Sunday morning?
From the breakfast window
my daughter and I watched
the flight in its fling,
soft shadow over the roofs
and down to feed,
knocking the sparrows off,
to take the seeds Mary and I
threw in sheets covering the porch.
What poise, precision of heavy beak,
the yellow, white, brown feathers
bird country clean in our city
of old snow.
There it was, the flock,
one sentry out, and grosbeaks walked
the quadrangle of the porch
robes drawn, precise, correct,
until they had done with us.

Warblers

Warblers,
dinghies in air,
bob in the branches,
tack with each
tickle of wind
around the garden,
prefer the apple tree,
nudge for food in the bark,
fidget, fret
fly north, south,
after each touching down,
for hardly longer
than a smile takes.

Swifts

The chitter of swifts —
in little strokes
they weave the sky
in fours and fives,
ideographs,
the sky takes
their marks,
and I would remember them,
and as from stone,
would take
a rubbing
to have as part
of this June's past.

Into the swamp

The mad shallows
at turtle dawn:
the darting time,
the canoe slips
on the water top
and I glide it
so close underneath
to shadowy schools,
sand clouds in
underwater piles
and the shadows grow
into thin light
in the waveless place
and what the swamp
echoes bring are
heron, bittern
and the long hidden
fight prolonged
going on
just underneath.

In the summer woods — I

The government scotch
is cheaper
and the name brand
they have disguised
this month
tastes like Teacher's to me.
In the woods
for the next month,
and we will count the rain,
while the mosquitoes
continue
to leap from the long-wet woods,
but we are in the woods,
and the river is there,
and it is one year later,
but we have come back
as yesterday,
as natives
with our boxes from the IGA
and beer
and enough staples to keep
the night cold out;
it is sun and shadow,
we really see
the pattern,
and Thoreau looks good,
and I begin with him again,
while the kids play cards.
"Sorry" is the name of their game,
and it always has been the name
of a game,
but lumps of thought
fill only the small crevasses;
where we scrape moss away,
the whole green and black
and sudden surprise
of colour of beetle and mushroom
give us a go
in these woods,

where questions and answers
give way to games for children,
a kind of coping
and glory, glory,
love, love, love.

In the summer woods — II

This month
bruised with hard sun,
swabs of heat followed by
blows of thunder
footing down the hills
where the river moves;
a holiday, the woods taking us
in, as it were,
and we adjusted,
the woods, squirrels, groundhogs,
people, birds,
the place steadied down,
became at times even familiar,
when quiet or storm,
a sudden light between leaves,
caught a pause in us,
just as one night there was
low cloud, heavy task of weather,
blocking stars,
just a clearing wind for mosquitoes
and we sat outside
by one candle's light,
drinking cider
smoking, talking, feeling.
And, ever after
we watched for another night
like that one
but none came
we looked on it as
a bonus, a timing lucky
in our lives —
candle, cider, the lumbering silence
of low cloud, so still,
and every once
one of us would wander off
to pee,
and what witnesses —
we knew them all
in the warm corridors of hemlock,
cloud, dark, woods,
the black river.

Open wide a wilderness

I

Open wide
a wilder-
ness

with hemlock
balsam
dense

worm bark
for nut-
hatches

black and
white
warblers

veerie thin
silver from
silence

the paths
shrink
inward

mushrooms
push
old leaves

overnight
they
erect

& there are
windless
nights

for sitting
taking
cider

taking close
ways of
wods

unto us,
wrap too
the night

the river
hill
touching

stars, a
meteor
once

told children
in one
hot fling

all there
is
to know

in black book
of
universe

black book
of all
things.

II

The open
wilder-
ness

each visit
each
year

each
a beginning
and closing

new terms
new shapes
of selves

& deeper we
dance
into

the maze
the
creeping

path so
unlike
anything

into soft
centre
labyrinth

gold maze
silver
flutes

birds on
a simple
casket

my parts
are
one

we are
to blink
and die

some minute
some now
in

the labyrinth
the tick-tock
wood

& what do
you say
to all

this open
and close-
ness

our shadow
dance where
damp limbs

piled and
rotting
lie

so much
like
half-tones

close-ups
of the world's
dead.

III

Then there is
the
book black

untouched
unopened
unread

so much
a cage
of gold

hiding a
devil bird
living

on pheasant
heads
but,

O, this wilder-
ness
opens

and closes
like pages
and covers

& strange
faces
portray

lurkings
& dark clouds
closed paths

the central
wilderness
labyrinthian

now grasps
for
death

it was all
too
easy

to find

to find
this dark centre
of labyrinth.

Luke Fox

Luke Fox, 1610,
or thereabouts
hanging around in Hudson Bay
looking for harbours,
wine-eyed beautiful Elizabethans
under command of —
          one is tempted to call him,
Old Luke, or something like that,
striding deck, bow-legged,
born on a horse, jeans,
feeling for the fabulous
up there, north, in uncertain seas
in a country without steeples,
without supporting ranges,
only sky and undulation
and cold gripping cold
and Luke calling the shot.

Luke, Luke
for dessert frozen delight
we look you
down the alleys of centuries,
cold, cold,
tell us of your God, Luke.
Out of the cold dank breath
of the unrelenting Bay
something resembling stone
no harbour
but hopes of the rigger men
Luke and his crew
shivering in their boots
felt for land to walk upon
found only a stubborn place
a landfall he reckoned
was nothing better
than "Hopes Checkt"

Two poets read in the King's Library, British Museum, May, 1967

The King's Library,
(Milton's *Commonplace Book* for instance), &
before the listening statue of the great Will,
one poet, thick-necked full-back
from Yorkshire, reads.
He never once looked up from his book,
following each line with finger,
(we all knew of his personal tragedy)
and he almost wept;
then the other, neat,
blue suit and shirt and tie
moustache, tidy, punctual,
(business and poetry go together)
he was chewing a little pill,
Tums.

In the King's Library
there were plotted plants,
a display of poets,
portraits of D. Thomas, V. Watkins,
their manuscripts,
and in the audience
live poets, one
with an Indian girl in yellow sari,
daisy in black hair,
(God, what beauty).

The girl standing in front of me
was wearing a bandaid
on her left heel,
and shifted in her shoe.

Unicorn in captivity — a 16th century tapestry

Tapestry of a unicorn
and flowers,
one of a series
made for A.B.,
a king's bride, surely.

Drawing a virgin
from their gamebag,
crafty hunters would bait trap,
and from behind trees
would watch her, until
with quick dart from wood
Mr. Unicorn would leap
into her lap, one embrace,
one touch,
then hunters would net him
for themselves.
This was in earlier times
when unicorn was held
to be very small,
like kid, but very fast,
only to be caught
by hunter's strategem.

When this tapestry was made
unicorn was horse,
white beauty, majestic,
but collared and tied
to orange tree no thicker
than his horn, captured
for a queen-to-be.
Caught, he is portrayed
fenced in, alone,
no bait, himself
the centre,
and his stage
a forest bank
of buttercup and columbine,
larkspur and wild rocket,
pink and gold fume-root,
fairy candles,

woodland flax
and Dutchman's breeches,
yellow and purple candy root,
wild four-o'clocks,
firewood,
and wand loosestrife.

This unicorn
for the queen-to-be
is content:
the flowers are his
farthest world and universe.
He knows their wild colours
and rare fragrance
set forth his whiteness
and his storied horn is there
to reach the centre of the sun
if he desires.
But in this tapestry
he simply waits
to be admired,
a contented prisoner.

Disguises

You talk
and
you wear
such strange
disguises.

Out
from behind
jumps love,
(I translate it
that way),
and talk
becomes wind,
draws flame
and your
disguises
burn.

You are you
again;
love a
blooming cherry
in a green
distance.

I talk to,
take you,
throw you
down, as
you knew
I would.
You and your
disguises.

Louie

I

Bear-happy, squaw-loose Louie
in a big winter wind,
authentic life in a clearing,
like sweat and foot foot
through the stiff north he knew
running once, walking

crossed himself before thoughts.
Do I care who is in the snare?
Do I club the beggar in the trap,
or does he club me?
It is too cold to ask. I whack
the beggars when they move.

Bear-happy humpy Louie
this blast, this cold, is all yours Louie.

II

I bolts the door and licks
my scrapes, my toes they thaw
between her thighs   my squaw
she is fourteen   scratch

Who knows what her lone wait for Louie is?
What ding dong does in this old shack
my pot-bellied warmth & her hard
charms endure the night, outlast the storm.

Breed, breed the wild dream says
our priest dances with a mini,
my squabble in heaven
will play real hell with the harps.
That's me, Louie.

III

O my whiskey Louie, trapper of bears,
windy lover, snow stomper, squaw chaser,
we met this zero-cracking day,
north of Wascasu.
Someone had hiccups eating sausages.
You kissed your squaw,
and what could she do then,
but take the winter draughts,
and wash your drawers?
The big man-toss talk and drink we had Louie,
and your lies and mine about life-love
stood high as the quick, green, polar shafts of light.
O my whiskey Louie, trapper of bears, windy lover,
up there, north of Wascasu.

Étienne

Étienne Brûlé — what in hell happened?
I can only ask your ghost, take him out,
drink wine in some private smoke-pit.
What in hell up there? What in hell down there?
". . . probably the first white man . . . to see
lakes Huron, Ontario, Superior, and Erie
. . . murdered by the Hurons, June 1633."

"he left no personal description . . . ." He
shoved off, like Rimbaud maybe?
Étienne into the woods, traded to the Algonquin chief,
you became interpreter (truchement)
walking Huron dictionary. First one,
you heller, to shoot Sault-Saint-Louis;
first one to take the torture
from the Iroquois. Did you,
did you not talk miracles when a storm
threw bullets on your enemy?
but no wonder with all that torture, white water,
you were, they say, ". . .viscious and much addicted
to women". Okay for that
but what in hell out there — they eat you
after you were twenty years a brother.
It was the Bear Tribe of the Hurons.
The woman scholar who writes your battered story
puts in all the details, all the bones
she can find.

The cemetery at Loch End, Catalone, Cape Breton

Long grass of summer held back by wire fence
but on the inside it was all fresh cut
and we did not think, then, of what stroke
or, whatever, cut the sleepers down who lay
beneath, but we were respectful, careful,

walking along the rows of leaning headstones
in our kangaroo jackets and sneakers damp
with sea-dew where the lawn's path led us on
to read inscriptions, to say the names and ages
out loud, repeating almost chanting on the morning wind.

There was only the cut-back forest and passing
tourists bound for Louisbourg and out beyond
fog and sea, hidden as the sleepers were. It
was that way as we knelt and touched with fingers
the lichen bitten lines of those graven images.

And for one Sarah Jane: "What I say unto you,
I say unto all, watch". We as watchers
made note of the marble and the message,
and one John Nicholson said: "Take ye heed, watch and
pray for ye know not when the time is".

When we prepared to leave we were quiet
there at Loch End. We had been told to wait,
to watch, to pray, but not to weep for them,
for those Presbyterians in Catalone,
Sarah Jane and Katie, Alex, Neil and John.

Uncle Amos
for Jack and Anna Van Wart

I don't remember your death.
I remember you alive
You are back again
in the same kitchen doorway,
(the outside kitchen)
of your sister's house,
my grandmother,
so you are not even my uncle
but in the family
and you can be nothing else
to me, than Uncle Amos.

Those were minutes we had
in July visits in the Thirties,
in New Brunswick,
when you drove the wagon
in from Scotch Settlement,
90 degrees on an average noon
in your black serge suit
with a week's find of eggs,
but you must have hidden
the overalls you wore at market,
made a quick change into serge,
in the men's of the City Hall,
red brick and bars,
and then relieved, you came to visit—
your eggs and whiskers
and giant mitts of hands
and stood six-six
until you took the lid off your week's
silence with a belly-laugh
you brought all the way in
from Scotch Settlement.

Even the church is gone up there—
but the view from the horse-shed
away down over the island and the river
was your spectacular, you never
mentioned it, but now I know—
and stoop in the grass of the cemetery
to find your stone
it sleeps with the others, the sisters,
brothers, fathers, mothers,
all the Sarahs! and
with some I must sponge
green and orange lichen
from the headstones.

To begin with 1826, with all the Mitchells
and you were Amos
and the farm days fell
beneath your boots
and when and what was love,
warmth, the Sunday in your soul,
the necessary evil, and
who was the passion for your thighs?

The burdocks, daisies, buttercups
become your lost farm,
the clearings sloping sunward,
but, there is a wind to blow,
to blow the dust from the leavings of your house,
only the cellar forms are there.

They tell me you were the last to go.
The farm, what happened?
I am the only owner under God.
The latest to see your grave.
What to do now but listen for
the lost folktales of Amos
drift once more
on these very winds.

the poems I mean to say

will someone
please forget
that this is
a party
and just come
in and have
what poem he
likes and failing
that, please taste
my blood as it
sprays, cascades
all over them,
over falls, rocks,
days of now
or never
over loves and
lays and words,
the poems I
mean to say?

Bandy-legged poem

Take it

you bend it
the way
you want it

I give it
the way
I see it

touch etc
and you
wiggle

go stark hairy
in your
under-

wary neck fuzz
creeping
straight out

spring fuses
routs
shouts, etc

Bandy-
legged
poem

dead gull

What is it?

grey blue white and black
while the lake
throws up a small sea
and wind comes in
on beginning combers

the elements,
your elements,
conspire, dead gull

dead-set your body
is already eye-less,
the past of searching
gone, probably,
your inland gliding
to fields and dumps

dead gull on narrow strip
of beach, I mourn

dead gull
spreading my arms over you
they make a shadow
of flight

but with what sun
there is,
my body and arms
build a dissolving cross,
a black stain of mourning
over your hard place —

The rogue wave

Forward and back
    the days seem simple
with death
    and change:
this land freezes,
    the wind beckons snow,
the eyes wait,
    the seeing is wide
with December sky
    with few birds
except here and there
    a stir
of snow buntings
    finding old seeds
in old pods
    near a barn
in a hollow.
    but what is simple
in my slumping days
    is clouded with the thud
of upright loves, stuffed tears:
    it is the queasy time
of the rogue wave
    the strafing one,
the rogue wave hitting
    the hull of my live,
as it smacks all of us
    in its way
and stays, in the eye,
    in the ear's bell,
in the banked fire
    of our rage,
in these simple days
    of death and change.

Credo

From the water faces we have seen
emerge, make noises, become whales
in our vision, running our world
from day to day —
are we forced to believe? Yes.

I believe in birds, books, beer and bees;
I believe in cats, dogs (their certain directness I like);
I believe in the tough legacy of the old poets;
       ancestors and cranberries;
I believe in Scullion and Plager, two bullies;
I believe in words found in air, in moments,
       hands scraping on tombstones;
I believe the view I see from anywhere, in
          the leaf my hand holds, the promise
          of auroras;
I believe the world is a poem, diamond,
       the light burning through it, changing;

Yes, I believe we go on, life and death,
       around and around,
       faces and ripples,
       faces and ripples.

Are you writing any . . . ?

And, yes, as
a matter of fact,
yes,
I am, I am
all the time,
and if you want
to know the truth
when I am not writing it,
I carry it.
But to find it,
I draw
a circle
all around it,
but let me tell you,
there are problems —
you must find it,
and be good
at circles.

Samuel Hearne's Bloody Fall at Pickering Beach

Bloody Fall,
against the Coppermine
where Samuel Hearne
stood in the hacking middle
of massacre;
his Indians
as butchers of Eskimaux,
and Hearne himself,
after warning them
felt the tremor of death
lick his moccasins
and he was lucky
to come out of it;
somehow this beach
this day
brings red into my eyes
and all the past and present suffering
falls heavy.

Gull from microworld

this night
you take this book
these pages

gull what pushes you
against my sleep
my lying here
inshore

while you bring
your offshore island
certain walk
and stride me
under
settling down
quick grabbing
dangerous
stuffing wings
under
you have taken over
made a nest
of my place
before my ruddy eyes

your trumpet scream
fills my night
my plague of you
in delirium
shouts back
but your scrounging
your head the room back
laughs me sick

what bait bags
did bring you here
your down wind down
enfolds me
you brace
my eye falls
as you turn
in this room
my God
strange strange joy
in this bird's breast

The herring gull
Larus argentatus

against stone
against beach log
against sticks
against jackstraw tumble
against wave
against sky
against sea stretch
against wind
against storm
against sun
against beach
against sand
against family
against day
against blood
against sinew
against fisherman
against world
against death
against
against

from *High Marsh Road*
October 1

night. damp. the black cougar was sighted.
several miles from here into the marsh
where there are tamarack and spruce.
the forests of the night cougar

2

this morning cold. what awakened
me to it were the sounds of
the rum-dipped duck hunters
firing in broken bursts

3

the clouds are beyond fetching, and
beyond the blind hunters. beyond
all the mouths whose lips smell of
corruption. it is their mindless
conspiracy to kill. to kill with
as much as a glare, the innocents,
the good ones. this is what
gets me down

4

the matching petals. how alike;
as I come closer your breasts
are almost motionless but the
shadows, textures and tones make
differences

5

the time to rest the eyes and fling
them far like stars. they fall on
the marsh and become mushrooms
for other people to pick up

6

light glances on the puddles along
the High Marsh Road. October about
this time of the month is for
geese and they continue to fly high,
very high. I have seen none touch
down this autumn

7

it is the morning to see a Rousseau
sun. the wide marsh takes the
long rays as they push up
details of grasses, wild birds
(wilder somehow in this place because
it is so much theirs). so many things
emerge with the orange light of it

8

the real round of the saying never forms,
but the poet is constantly working, moulding
it closer and closer to the truth

9

the total glimpse of it as Roberts
took to Tantramar. using his telescope
his eye revisited. now I search the
same dykes for details of shore-birds.
the weirs hold straggler ducks. it is
good to have such footsteps

10

at once it was good. our meeting
solitary in a hospitality room full
of noise. yes it was very good.
the walking in utter quiet brings
it all back. good

11

dear x.
       you have made notes to put into a letter.
this you told me. you are afraid that
whatever you say will give the wrong
emphasis. will encourage me. lead me on.
I am my age and I listen to all of this.
it *does* make sense. you want to avoid
hurting me who now hide behind three-foot
walls. yes, once I did get the wrong
idea and I let it take off. leading to
nothing. I don't mind. nothing hurts
anymore. this you must tell yourself.
please write

12

the colours take over. long
banners of green, white and hard blue
stream into abstractions. in the
fog the marsh vanishes

13

the number of times I have said yes.
non, non et non. my mouth is
already formed

14

I give way. crawl inside
myself. the thought of such
ruling bastards troubles my
innocence. this must stop.
remember your age

15

another day. anguished muscles
of cloud and wind drive me to
ground. I lie in an empty field.
only dreams are warm

16

the poet. yes. but taken apart who
is this lurcher, lecher, big bear talker,
bull in a word-shop? when the mirror says
so much, I hesitate to look at the remains
of the others. fellow poets rot with me

17

the continual measuring. wishing for
otherwise. the great game of 'if'. no,
it could not be me but Harry. the hands
of the world close on all of us into
fists and we are nut shells

18

these are my fifties. never have I
been so aware. so clear about it.
every day (and night) new disguises.
over the familiar (unknown?) face grows
a strange mask. the lines harden.
deepen. a crazy grid in so many directions

19

this is my place. it is for me to tell
you. coming from inside. the mind
is not enough. I must take all
signals. events. the accident
at any moment can wreck worlds.
yours and mine

20

the wild frenzy for life. the streaming
constellations make statements I fail
to hear night after night. the blind and
the deaf and the fight going on in the
crush of silence

21

I move with the harrier. the mole
is my nestling lover. roots I trace
and cover myself with the green
and brown rot. what face to see,
to write down? each feature a
mockery. a saint unfolds. there
is a wild marriage of detail. who
will arrange it? it is my doing

22

the same wind. without such great measures.
how do I bring such details for all to see.
in this basket of your skirt? underneath
the details continue. what brought you five
thousand miles for this? why questions?

23

your visit was all planned.
my own disney land. to show
you marsh. find a harrier. buy
lobster. take wine. these
would be our observances. rituals
before love. a dirty dragging
hope it all was too. where the
hell did you go?

24

sea time. out there is Chignecto. in from
it the tidal grasses are wind-churned on
Tantramar. skitters of shorebirds

25

first frost to kill. there is not
much left on the marsh. a hint of
ice in ruts. the mists will not
burn off until ten. then the cold
feel of it will be gone

26

you will give me a shotgun.
the ammunition I already have.
you will go along that side.
I will cover this. I will
throw my ammo and all into the river.
this is my plan

27

the fields are raw. goldfinches
are after seeds. they keep the
place alive. who is there with me
to watch their bouncy-flight?
they are busy until dark

28

thin snow lying almost until noon
then lapsing into green. the first
fall came in the night. I did
not see it but I did hear the
geese high and honking. telling,
telling

29

I arrived late. over there three ducks
in worried flight. the stars dominate.
some are heavy with light. a comfort
of dark. the strange embrace of it

30

a golden plover, then another.
solitaries but together. their
sudden drama. at least as I see
it. will they get past the hunters?
they only understand buckshot.
stalk them in their pickup trucks
and shave them with a shot

31

yes, but something will turn up.
something will come of it all. the
road will remain. echoes of all
this picked up. Charles G.D.
Roberts, pince-nez and tails, flies
like an angel by Stanley Spencer over
this place

The Cottage

We have just arrived. The cottage opens to the sea. The beach runs in both directions only a stone's throw. The sea is at first a fumbling background. A building, blowing noise which will take over our first night. But now is the time to unpack. We choose beds. Maybe one will do. I want to get my feet in sand, I said. Don't try to take it all in at once. Murphy — Irish. How long have they been here? This always seems to matter. Another look to where the sea runs. More orderly this look from high on left to distance to right. What is distance? The long horizontals of it. Who is on the beach? A dog runs in a tangle of smells. He goes from one mark to another. Nose keeping him from running himself ragged with all that sand. The lips of water make sucking noises. We are here.

Two Rows

Tonight I planted two rows of potatoes. Long rows for a backyard garden. Cut each in half. Two eyes. Twelve inches apart. Eighteen apart. I chose twelve because I had too many. Wally, who knows what it is all about, helped me. Two furrows pushed deep enough using a rake-handle. Slice potatoes — Done. Some bending and groans. Now to cover. First I stepped on each spud pushing it down a bit. Then pulling each over with rake. Nothing to it Wally said. Wait until August. As I filled the trench, stepped on the potatoes, and felt the red dirt, fairly dry for this time of year, I really did say, if it needed saying, that this is why I came here. To plant two rows on such a night in June. Sun just over the trees behind the Quarry and clouds with a moon. New. Two rows. Not too much mind blowing. Just right.

Big Bud of Glace Bay

Resembling a trial. Some kind of probation. We sleep, waken, go softly grim, hard. And what are you? I am a drone, gnome, poet, pitcher, peever. And what do I hear? Isn't that too bad. Too bad. This from the hand-hewer of life, the big Bud-boy drinker of a couple of quarts and a double on the noon whistle break. Big Bud now dead. Big man capable of igniting the wire, dropping walls of coal down on a dime. He never beat his wife but he kicked a hole in the parlour wall. Life is a narrow stair. Up and up. Down and down. The mine shaft is black, the members of the establishment adjust helmets. Only the wives look at the stars and curse-curse, "Holy Father this Friday I know I didn't mean it."

Trip

I sit in the god-given city. The love is a newfoundhippieland understood in their under-nourished grinning faces. The stunned son of the hard-nose dean leans on his tender trip against a gigantic elm. The boy is dream until you pick him up and rush him to Emergency. The tree is quite dead with Dutch elm disease. Where the branchs meet trunk, in the armpits, kneebends and crotches the woodpeckers bang at the weevils. So, in his, the son's wobble-walk the holes are bored in the angles of his eyes, the brain clouds and there are no holes but our hope. All this happening this counting time on a heavy street, with leaden houses and doors. Emergency.

Louisbourg

Go the given trail. I stand at this harbour entrance. White blue white. Gulls against sky. Moving cormorants bark. The putt-putts push into harbour. Louisbourg still with its fill of old cannon in the shifting bottoms. The cold frozen starved 18th century French in the fog-lined place. The stone bastions restored. Blue and green glass. One million smashed wine bottles. Wine to stun the cold out.

Beausejour

The sun has been at it all day. Warm. Now breezes bring words of
night in from the bay. Out there. Marked by slow slides of land on
either side which trace the Fundy's path in towards shore. So it is.
The time is too early for tourists. Few footsteps on the new green
of old mounds where rubble of men and death and rock lie piled.
About it there were times of war. Of ships bringing irregulars who
captured the place from regulars. Bullets. What is that shining in
the turf just over there while you think of it? The ground
everywhere slopes away, including the dead sleeping mounds of
fort, onto the fire-darkened early May fields burnt. Some still
smoking. Now black. The lines running as streamers are fences,
dikes and across the middle distance the main railway line. They
intersect bringing their own order. We belong here now. But
once twenty, thirty more likely years ago we stopped, my parents,
my brother and I, and to break the trip we sat on the same
benches, followed the same directions, the same fence
dimensions and there before my eyes I saw a fox, going over low
ground, around water patches, not running but aware and ready.
"Yes, 'tis a fox" he said, and I said, "Yes, its tail. Watch the tail!" No
fox to bring new tracks. He was as red then as the sun. Strong
outline leaning with purpose. The sun now is overhead and away
to west. Over the fox-field where the old fort is.

The meeting

I went that way
     walking the bitten beach
     of this half-winter:

only the headland
     and the shifts of light
     building others into it

until at last I found
     on looking down, a spade-handle
     a hand carved artifact

of some bending toiler
     gone unknown somewhere
     and this was his leaving

my hands felt the hand
     which made and used it
     to make a walkway of dyke

and into this force of past
     I let myself in
     and talked to him for days.

The poem

the poem if it goes soft
    leads into itself
    into a place of mirrors

and to lift it up
    is to see soft presences
    of profiles, of strangers

and shifting slides
    not quite in focus
    of friends and foes

where some sun lives,
    or has lived, bringing
    new traces, new places

and what is held up
    to all of this, the poem
    tells its story

soft, unfolding, a morning flower
    turned out and up
    into a softer telling.

A matter of time

it is only a matter of time
given one high tide

and the land will shake loose
clearing out the silt's century

and at low tide there will be
old adzes and saws of lost men

who turned up regular and built
ships for trading from this bay

it has all gone, but will come back
in old log books, accounts of companies

in the sun's memory of slips
shouts and ropes licking the wind.

Voices

the voices call from out there
whirlpools in the fathom-throat

of the wide place of sea
the long silent pushing and pulling

of tides and the moon moving
the ragged leavings, codes on beaches

so do the grains build into the flesh
of the wet hard body;

there is no ending, stopping
the tide-marsh bleeds with the wind

and the marks are there
or the lickings and lashings of it.

Mud flats, Rockport

the marshes move into long narration
of distance, it is not all easy

going as they shift chapter by chapter
through lines laid down, taken up

by the Chignecto winds, by winds beyond there
by testaments of cloud coming over

it is too soon to translate the markings
somehow made by some great mould of sky

laid down now on the caught sand
inlaid with snow and strewn water

the message lies a pattern and heavy
waiting for one who can read it.

Questions

what is left from the warm and wine dark sea?
and what is there before the eye?

the gamble-toss of wasted things
brought forth from clearing decks

from the lagging losses of fragment days
where sailors dock their souls and socks

the dark red place of mud and mix
the gone gulls grate on other skies

done in a whip of wind and scream
where are they now? but no voice asks.

there are questions incised in mud and rock
there are questions blowing at sea-time.

To remember a landscape here

to remember a landscape here
how do you handle it?

looking out a sudden glance of curlew
a way of shining, a cloud's presence,

it is something like opening the Bible
beginning somewhere in quiet or tumult

such as the land looked wide and hard
held down by the preaching presence

of some greater silence, or did it pitch away,
looking like leavings from some giant chef's

daring tracery decorating something
to be looked upon in wonder?

Collage

a crazy collage, a hand-dipped chocolate
stamped with wild wedges, cracked logos

of a thousand sneakers, and giant biting gnats
in some unknown, unseen ritual, they did dance

on this likely place, exhausted with their whining
and walking, the gnats gave way to mincing moles

then gluttonous gulls, foot-stomping steamers
placing their webbed soles in gull-grip

so did these shapes shift into place for now
so did the oyster shells make their pattern

now they are gone except the wedged-wildness
of their dance, frozen in sandstone shapes.

Ice-flowers

At Aulac a sudden field of ice-flowers
their perfume of steam sprays the world

the February air. Now the marsh is ice
in a breaking, hardening hand-hold,

change is sudden, subtle, going on always
where the dykelands loosen and lock

and it was that winter when a Snowy Owl
made winter camp on a sculptured pole

giving out its presence with silence
and with quick talon-tricks he kept

the place alert, all Aulac knew
and he stayed the breaking winter out.

Views I and II

a play of fields

*

over there: some distance
a play of fields

with light somehow
falling on and around

it is in the centre
of it, the light

pivot of change
doubling the eye

trembling into itself
without shape

**

so that it is there
a shifting place

a delicate statement
a rough decision

made up of fields
and half a sky

but against the centre
unable to pick up

or examine, unable
to talk dimensions

the walk towards it
goes on and on

***

there, not as far as it was,
but now is flatness

a streaming out of form
a softening place and light.

It is not anymore, all
as sudden as field-death

now only the fog contains,
contains all, a flood

of taking away, now
an absence holds.

Tracks

from the TransCanada the tracks of snow and hay
point as fingers at the tailored towers

of the CBC. This spring is one of messages
and while the snow's crazy abstract grows

a Polish commentator in Montreal this day
sends his toiling words to Warsaw and Gdansk,

an Italian sings and through the splits of towers
there are sounds in Amalfi and Palermo

so the many messages of men give out
their vibes to make a homesick noise

around the world from this brooding marsh
where mole and mouse take cover in their place.

Hard statements

the hard statements of bridge and rail
lines of poles and the staggered fences

all give the hard edge of man's plotting
patterns, of his unsubtle strictures

over the great marshes. Their short lives
seem unbelievable but it is a fact,

the land is a waiting enemy, it possesses
all the lasting virtues, while rust runs

in increasing rivers over its Madonna face
and the crash and crackle of trains are heard

going somewhere, the place is there
and it is only a minor question, really.

Strange gestures

it is somehow significant every second
a heaving and hustle of all our change

taking the Bible's constant use of, say,
mystery, mysterious, even the scientist

coming home with a bevy of test tubes
filled with new silt for weighing

it is, here, a case of nature's writing
leaving strange gestures of land and light

there is really nothing for man
in the presentation and play of it,

such as now, the measure of snow here
tracing the fields and sky to unknown limits.

Dyke at Dorchester Cape

a man he went and got the others
and with what was there got down to it

plunging the staying stumps into the soup
of red mud and somehow made them hold

it was on a first day, give or take
when they began, another when they finished,

so at Dorchester Cape the summer talk
of dust and dried grass and noise of lunging lovers

ripping by, the dykes are necessary ruins
part of the hump and beginning ridge

they lift up the place, keep it tight
against the drop and haul of sea

Ditch on the Marsh, Aulac

a sudden wound, a heavy sex,
and the marsh lies rich and wanton

bare as she waits open
for the questing hand and plunge,

but, as always, this in only part
of the heady show of dyke and ditch

the earth is whored out to farmers
who feed her until she bursts

their barns with hay, it is their taking,
it is natural, it is their time

of rounding it into balls and bales
and hiking heaves into the lap of harvest.

The Remains of the Bridge, Dorchester

out there the cold remains of pilings
in a winter-waiting tide

the strength, the order, a kind of love
is shared as each to each

the pilings on an inward morning
stand as shattered sentries, almost,

and then the clopping traffic
of the near past batters the ear

the leaning tense figures with reins
and the horses adding white breath

in the bridge's close. The sides and roof
went last year, an October tide it was.

From Mount Whatley Road

looking down from Mount Whatley, at a certain place,
there the roughed-in trees and farms

take the middle distance, established stations
looking out with a full-faced permanence

to the careful striking of the foreground weeds
against the laid paper of snow

to far tongues of sea and promontories
their placed lives set the stage

and it is enough today, talking
to unseen faces out there and there

for the talk is soft in this pencilled stage
and the world from Whatley is a winter place.

At Jolicure

wind was here but gone now, an instant,
and what remains is written in stocks

where corn waved to ordinary skies
and held fast a summer marsh

now at Jolicure the land is joined
in a waiting game, marsh traces,

then tracks of geese, new lines and wedges,
will scrape the space with their travelling show

and what is sure are the steady faces
of the sentry barns keeping their chosen places.

the striped fields back into the sky
and await their marching messages.

Near Dorchester

the carved carcass of the tide's leavings
the chocolate rocks and wooden pilings

the whole heaped and tired assembly
of the bay's gut hangs heavy

the jam of rock, the key-block blown loose
and the entrails shift in red waters

it is a time of trying, the old bridge
was its own creaking coffin gone sour

the local terrors beat it down
with souped-up Chevs held fast by chrome

where have the boyos and the old bridge gone?
they have gone to sleep in the sea's throat.

A brief whiff

what snow there was came as accident
a brief whiff of it in from Fundy

but the dimensions harden and the cut field
holds the thin white of it, a consistent plaster

of finding dust over the forgotten criss-cross
and toilings of men and tractors hauling

themselves through centuries of seasons
with minds gone to their very edges

and hard the sea-soaked flats glisten
with the hint of it, the time of winter

and whisps and belts of snow and ice
the pits and pores on the skin of it.

From Fort Lawrence Road

only itself, the wide reading of it
looking west from Fort Lawrence Road

the winter snow is in its rich possession
is sudden on a December morning

packed and pulled by sea wind
the light slowly pricks it into life

bringing out the bristles of a weekend face
suggesting a welter of wrinkles frozen

hard on the aging land, but no, the land waits,
the marsh has been this way before

the route of age means nothing, only the grip
is sure, sure of the coming change.

So close

Tantramar, the river, deep, tidal
moving on a March morning, high as she goes

there in the banked and thrown ice
the leaking limits of the marsh

move free in their melting, leaving crusts
to the shudder of tidal might.

The sea-force moves and makes a landscape
empty in a winter season of searching birds,

it is a happening of nature we try to chart
and plot our way to nearer understanding

but it is the going on of the place
the floating-by of life, so close, so close.

A loud place

After first sight you look into the place
where details emerge like bubbles

the eye takes and reads in its own way:
there it is a long ride of rail

a trail of pulsing wind-warped poles
and a staked fence saying what fences say

now it is a place of meeting, retreating
of taking the message of nature and man

it is not an emptiness, but a loud place
for reading, for noting this and that

not forgetting the marsh mood
heightened by heavy and brooding skies.

Index of first lines